Published by Creative Education and
Creative Paperbacks
P.O. Box 227, Mankato, Minnesota 56002
Creative Education and Creative Paperbacks
are imprints of The Creative Company
www.thecreativecompany.us

Design by The Design Lab
Production by Chelsey Luther
Printed in the United States of America

Photographs by Dreamstime (Dpsmedia9,
Henkbentlage, Izanbar, Jamen Percy), Getty Images
(Alexandre Boudet, mcb bank bhalwal), National
Geographic Creative (KLAUS NIGGE), Shutterstock
(Anton Derevschuk, Erik Mandre, Wildnerdpix),
SuperStock (age fotostock, Kirill Kurashov, NaturePL,
Paul Souders/Alaska Stock-Design Pics)

Library of Congress Cataloging-in-Publication Data
Riggs, Kate.
Brown bears / Kate Riggs.
p. cm. — (Amazing animals)
Summary: A basic exploration of the appearance,
behavior, and habitat of brown bears, mammals
identified by their shoulder humps. Also included is
a retelling of the Greek myth about Ursa Major and
Minor.
Includes index.
ISBN 978-1-60818-487-3 (hardcover)
ISBN 978-1-62832-087-9 (pbk)
1. Brown bear—Juvenile literature. 2. Grizzly
bear—Juvenile literature. I. Title. II. Series: Amazing
animals.
QL737.C27R546 2015
599.784—dc23   2013051247

CCSS: RI.1.1, 2, 4, 5, 6, 7; RI.2.2, 5, 6, 7, 10;
RI.3.1, 5, 7, 8; RF.1.1, 3, 4; RF.2.3, 4

First Edition
9 8 7 6 5 4 3 2 1

AMAZING ANIMALS

BROWN BEARS

BY KATE RIGGS

CREATIVE EDUCATION • CREATIVE PAPERBACKS

Ten kinds of brown bears live in the world today. Grizzlies are some brown bears that live in North America. Other brown bears are in Europe and Asia.

*Grizzly, coastal,
and Kodiak brown
bears live in Alaska*

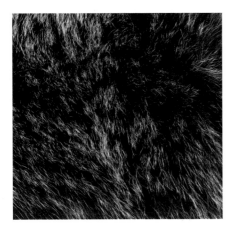

Brown bears do not always have brown fur. Sometimes their coats are black. All brown bears have a big hump near their shoulders. The hump is made of strong muscles.

Brown bears sometimes use their muscles to fight

Kodiak brown bears are the biggest brown bears. They live in cold places and eat a lot of fatty fish. Male Kodiak bears can be 1,500 pounds (680 kg). Other male brown bears weigh about 800 pounds (363 kg).

The world's largest brown bear weighed 2,130 pounds (966 kg)

Brown bears usually walk or run on four feet. They can run up to 35 miles (56.3 km) per hour. Bear feet and hands are called paws. Each paw has five claws.

The claws on a brown bear's paw are long and curved

Brown bears eat meat and plants. Most brown bears eat a lot of grass and berries. Brown bears can smell food from far away. They hunt animals like ground squirrels and deer. Some brown bears catch fish to eat.

Brown bears look for fish that swim in cold rivers

As many as four cubs can be born at once

A mother brown bear usually has two **cubs**. The cubs are born in a **den**. Bears spend the winter sleeping in dens. In spring, the cubs leave the den. They live with their mother for two to four years.

cubs baby bears

den a home that is hidden

There are not many Himalayan brown bears left in Asia

Adult brown bears live alone. Each bear has a **home range**. Brown bears can live up to 35 years in the wild. Bears in zoos can live even longer.

home range an area where animals live that has enough food for them to eat

Brown bears eat plants and look for other food. They walk around their home range. They like to rub their backs on trees. They use their claws to leave marks on trees, too.

Bears use the same "rubbing trees" over and over

Sometimes people see a brown bear in the forest. It is a good idea to make a lot of noise. Brown bears do not like surprises. Watch these big bears from a safe distance!

Hikers talk or sing to let bears know they are coming

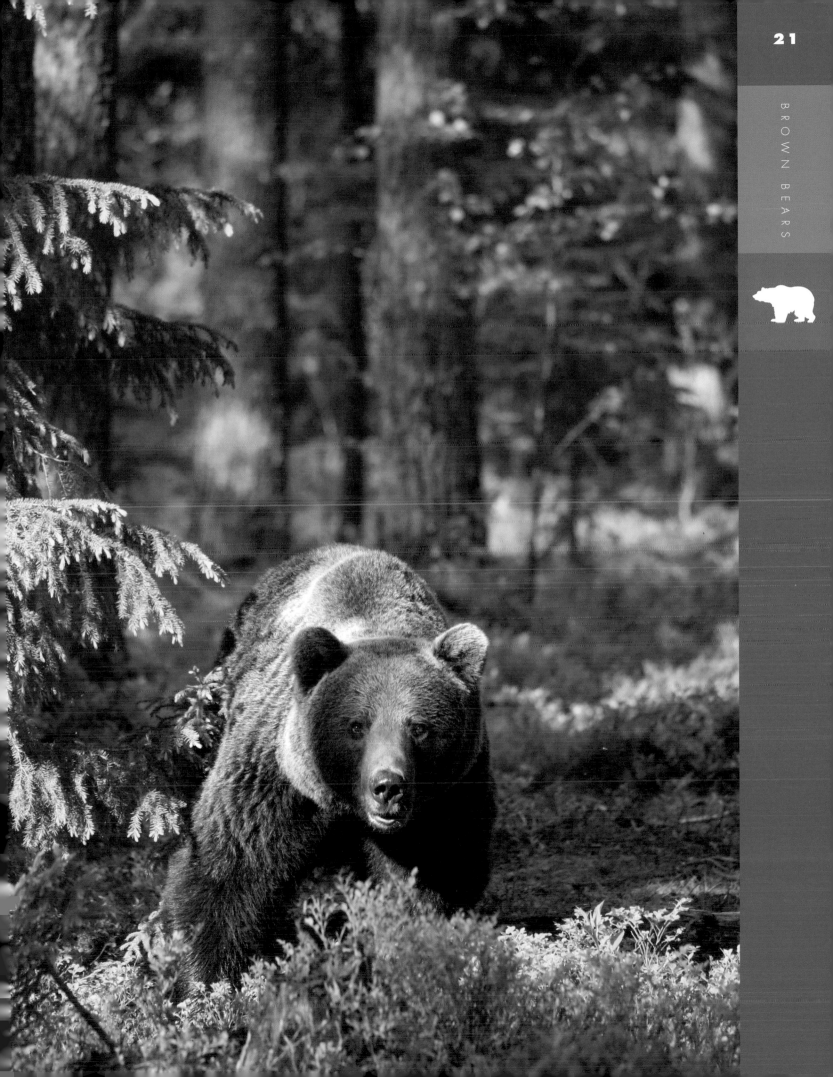

A Brown Bear Story

How did bears become stars? People in Greece used to tell a story about this. A woman named Callisto had a son, Arcas. A jealous goddess turned Callisto into a bear. One day, Arcas was hunting. He did not know his mother was one of the bears! The king of the gods put Arcas and Callisto into the sky to keep them both safe. That is how the Great Bear and the Little Bear became stars.

Read More

Owings, Lisa. *Bear Attack*. Minneapolis: Bellwether Media, 2013.

Wendorff, Anne. *Bear Cubs*. Minneapolis: Bellwether Media, 2009.

Websites

KidZone: Bear Activities
http://www.kidzone.ws/lw/bears/activities.htm
This site has activities about brown bears to print out.

National Geographic: Grizzly Mom Teaching Cubs
http://video.nationalgeographic.com/video/bear_grizzly_teachingcubs
Watch a video of a grizzly teaching her cubs to catch fish.

Note: Every effort has been made to ensure that the websites listed above are suitable for children, that they have educational value, and that they contain no inappropriate material. However, because of the nature of the Internet, it is impossible to guarantee that these sites will remain active indefinitely or that their contents will not be altered.

Index